REVELATION
The New Jerusalem is Now!

Wyatt House books may be ordered through booksellers or by contacting:

Wyatt House Publishing
399 Lakeview Dr. W.
Mobile, Alabama   36695

Because of the dynamic nature of the Internet, any web address or links contained in this book may have changed since publication and may no longer be valid.

Cover design by: Mark Wyatt
Interior design by: Mark Wyatt

ISBN 13: 978-1-7345398-4-4

Printed in the United States of America

REVELATION
The New Jerusalem is Now!

NEW
updated and expanded
EDITION!

by

MELVIN ROBINSON

Wyatt House Publishing

Wyatt House Publishing
Mobile, Alabama

A Note from the Author:

This study is intended to primarily give the overall context of the book of Revelation. Having said that, it should be a great book to study individually or as a class study to build upon. I do not go verse by verse, but each chapter of the book corresponds with its same chapter in Revelation. I encourage you to read the intended chapter in the Bible before reading the parallel chapter of this book. I hope it will increase your faith in God's amazing plan as we grow in grace and in the knowledge of our Lord Jesus. Christ.

Revelation:
The New Jerusalem is Now!

To have a better understanding of the book of Revelation, its message can be made clearer as we read other scriptures such as the parables that Jesus gives in Matthew 21:33-46, Mark 12:1-12 and Luke 20:9-18. A perfect picture of Revelation as so many prophets came to His people to receive produce but was rejected and even killed! Surely they would receive His son but He too was rejected and killed. A patient God now has enough and brings destruction to them, Israel. John does reveal a parable in John 10: 1-18 of the good Shepherd. This may be another side that we look at which is also very important. He was the good Shepherd and would die/lay down His life for His sheep. He says "I have other sheep, not of this fold, which I will bring with me". Then to be one fold with one shepherd. This tends to point to the coming of the "New Jerusalem" that would come after His death, bringing salvation to all men! Could it be significant that all of these were written not long before His death? Perhaps to be fresh on their minds giving them understanding that they have rejected and killed the good Shepherd! Also we see the prophecy of Jesus Christ in Matthew 23 & 24:1-35 which were about things to come upon that generation. Daniel's account can also be helpful, especially Chapter 12. Many other Old Testament prophets had shed light about the time of Christ coming in His Kingdom along with the destruction of the Jewish nation, its laws, even to the destruction of Jerusalem and God's temple. Old law could now be a hinderance as the everlasting kingdom had come as said would come, in that generation. Mark 9:1 and Acts 2. The old law had been nailed to the cross because of so much corruption and sin, having killed their savior and in God's perfect time to make it happen. In Matthew 24 He wrote when you see the abomination of desolation you need to flee to the mountains.

He said Daniel had written about it. Daniel 12:1-3 seems to be much about the destruction of the old Jerusalem to come in the days of Christ or the last days! This will bring vengeance for those prophets that they had rejected and killed. Do we need to think of Jesus too, a prophet under the old law, the Christ that they had slain? Surely that had put much guilt on them! Matthew 24 mentioned earlier, is scripture that will be looked back to a lot. Just a choice made as similar scripture can be found in Mark 13:1-31, Luke 21: 5-36, as they may not be referred to very much but with a similar revelation of prophecy.

WHAT WILL WE SEE IN CHAPTER 1?

Christ now rules from heaven! His Kingdom has come and He has a message for the Churches of Asia. His everlasting kingdom is for all men and for all time! He is about to come in the clouds with judgment against Israel to fulfill His prophecy. We see Him out among His Churches watching over them. He is the Christ and he has risen!

Chapter 1

Israel in the days of Roman rule was struggling with Rome over taxes and their rule. Rome had some wicked and prideful rulers and God would use them to bring Israel and Jerusalem to its end. Daniel pointed to these days and along with the prophecy of Jesus as he was about to die giving plenty of warnings in Matthew, Mark and Luke. Rome was about to end their rebellion! In Christs warning He said the tribulation that was coming upon them would be the worst to ever occur on the earth! Matt 24:21. He gave them a time frame for it to happen. He said it would come in that generation as some of you will be around to see it. Matt 24:30-34. Some 35 years later it began in lasted for 3 1/2 years, ending in A.D. 70. Finished, Rev 10:7. So most of the tribulation found in Revelation pertained to Israel's destruction and not about today or the future. Tribulation is mentioned again in chapters 20:7-9, as the devil is loosed and goes out to persecute Christians from all over the world. God says enough and the whole world is destroyed! This later tribulation could be going on now as our world is in so much turmoil and wickedness? So we need to be prepared and ready! That's not to say we won't suffer tribulation in our time or in the future! Another thing said to come in that generation was the Kingdom of Christ! Mk 9:1. Along with that prophecy it seems very hard for men to grasp or to understand, "the last days"! We now are in the 2022 year of the last days of Christ. Our calendars help us in the understanding of "these last days"! Heb 1:1-3, tells us we are in the "last days" as Christ has come to His throne to rule over us, His Kingdom, which is the "Church age". The teachings of Him and His Kingdom still applies to us today and forever as His Kingdom is so different as it is not of this world but heavenly and everlasting. John 18:36.

We have John, through an angel, revealing prophecy about things soon to take place. It's to Christians and his bondservants. Note: "prophecy" of Jesus Christ of things that are about to take place. He testified to the Word of God, the testimony of Jesus Christ, in all that he saw. Blessed is he who reads and understands this "prophecy" and heeds these words for the time is near! Almost seems to be urgent? This written to the Gentiles who now share the blessings of Christ, a promise that goes all the way back to Abraham. It's from the Almighty God who you now believe in, who is, who was, and is to come! This is also from the seven spirits or the eyes, Rev 5:6, before God as servants to help us in understanding this prophecy. Also from Jesus Christ who died and rose again to God's right hand who has released us from our sins. Our King, ruler of the earth, first born of the dead, now reigning on his throne. His kingdom has come (Mark 9:1 & Acts 2). This was promised long ago and has made us to be priest to God, the Father. This promise goes back to David in II Samuel 7:12-13. He is coming in the clouds with judgment and all will know and see him even those who nailed him to the cross. (Matt 24:32-34). You will know and understand it's a day of wrath and destruction, pain and crying for all of Israel. "I am God the Almighty, beginning and the end and who is to come". Put away your gods? The writer, John, living in the days of much persecution, writes the testimony of Jesus from Patmos. The Holy Spirit was working in him on the Lords Day which was a mighty sound as of a trumpet. Was telling him to write in the book what you see and send it to the Gentiles or the seven Churches of Asia, that which is now for all men and for all time. He turned to see the voice speaking to him and saw the seven lampstands /Churches. Among the Churches he sees Christ in the midst of them wearing a robe girded with a golden sash. He was pure and holy, white wool like snow. His all seeing eyes were like a flame of fire. His feet as burnished bronze, glowing in the furnace as He is everywhere among His people. His voice like many waters of many languages going out to all the world! Now unto all men. In his right hand he held seven stars/angels (vs 20). From His mouth came a message as from a two edged sword, which may praise or condemn you or in two different ways. His face as the sun, brightly shining with much light and powerful! John was overwhelmed at what he saw! So he fell down as dead!

Christ now comforts him saying don't be afraid "I am the first and the last", or I am God in Christ! Saying now, I was a man, was crucified, then arose, now living forever, now having the keys of death and Hades. As Matt 28:18 says "all authority has been given to me in heaven and on earth". Write these things down as they are about to take place and also the things that come after. Could be from chapter 4 and onward? May even be, the Kingdom to come (Mark 9:1) or the destruction of Jerusalem (Matt 24:34)? The mystery of the seven stars/angels to the seven lampstands/Churches. The number seven, a significant number in this book in the possibility about this message is for all the churches of Asia and the whole world around them for all times? Giving instructions of how they should live before God to please Him. The things that he likes and also the things that He hates.

WHAT WILL WE SEE IN CHAPTERS 2 AND 3?

We now begin to see the mysteries of his kingdom of which the seven churches were a part of with instructions and teachings of how they were to live in order to please Him and God. None of them were perfect but given the opportunity to change to become perfect before Him.

Chapter 2

Now he begins his messages to the seven churches of Asia. That could be typical of all churches even today? To the angel in Ephesus, from Christ, who has seen and knows their works, those eyes from 1:14. You do many good things yet you have left your first love! You must repent and be like you were at first or I will come and remove your candlestick. No longer considered a lampstand? Yes, I'm glad you hate that evil deeds of the Nicolaitans, I do too! So listen to what the spirit says! He that overcomes will have access to the tree of life which is in the paradise God. (Rev 22:1-5) This is to be part of the bride of Christ or the "new Jerusalem"! To the angel of the church at Smyrna from God the first and the last who had died and had risen from the grave. From God the son! Says you are struggling as you don't have much, but you are rich! There is much wickedness around you! Also you're about to be persecuted even to being put into prison.

You are to be really tested! It's not to last too long or a literal 10 days. So endure, even to death and you will receive the "crown of life"! Listen and understand, if you overcome you will not be hurt by the second death. Could be looking at 20:6 as those who had died and receive the promise of having avoided hell, which is the second death! Now to the Church at Pergamum. You do pretty well in such a wicked world around you where Satan dwells! Even one of you died because of his faith! You have some things that disappoint me! The teachings of the other gods is tolerated as some follow in their ways. You must repent or I will come against you in judgment. Better listen and you will be blessed if you do. I will give you a hidden manna, spiritual food so you will not hunger. (John 6:49-51)

To the Church at Thyatira, and to the angel. Says "I see all and am everywhere. I know your deeds and faith, service and perseverance". You are growing as your deeds are greater than at first. But, you tolerate Jezebel who leads people away from God/me. She must repent of her deeds or I come and deal her much hurt/ tribulation. Everyone is to know I'll come to bring judgment to her if she does not repent. To the rest who do not hold this teaching, I will put no more on you. Those among you that keeps My deeds to the end will be granted authority over the nations. I will give you the Morning Star, Jesus Christ, Rev 22:16, the light of the world and of the new day of the "New Jerusalem". (II Peter 1:19)

Chapter 3

To the angel of the church in Sardis from He who has the seven spirits/eyes and the seven stars/angels says: I know your deeds as my eyes are on you. You think you are alive and well but you are dead! You must awaken and strengthen the good that remains which is about to die. You have failed in your good deeds!

Repent as you know My will and what has been given to you! I will come as a thief as you won't see me or know it. There are a few that are faithful and worthy to walk with Him in white. He that overcomes is to have white garments/saved and his name in the "book of life". I will confess his name before God and His angels. You need to listen and pay close attention! To the angel of the Church at Philadelphia from Jesus Christ, the key of David, I am Deity! I see your deeds so I have put a door of opportunity before you. You have been faithful and have not denied me. I will make those of the synagogue of Satan/

the proud, wicked Jews/ to come and bow down before you. Would be to let them know that I love you, died for you and have come to save you, the Gentiles. Because you have been faithful I will reward you and keep you from the hour of testing/persecution that's about to come upon the whole world by the Romans. It's to happen very soon! So hold fast! If you hold on and are faithful you will be rewarded. You will become a pillar in my temple. I will write on you the name of my God, the name of the city of my God, the "New Jerusalem", which has come down out of heaven from my God and My new name! (21:2). The old city gone, with it's laws which could not give you this. This is awesome, listen to what the spirit says!

Now to the angel of the Church in Laodicea from Christ, the amen, the faithful and true witness, the creator of the world. Says I know all about you. I know your deeds and you are neither cold or hot. I can't stand it, I have to spit you out of my mouth! You say, I am rich, wealthy, with no needs! You don't know that I hate your condition! You are so sinful and lost! You need to buy gold from me which is so different! Invest in me! To be refined by fire/cleaning out all of your impurities so that you can truly come to be rich! Able to have sins gone, to wear white garments so that the shame in which you were involved will no longer be seen and eye salve to clear your eyes so you can see what true riches are. You will be disciplined, so be zealous and repent, it's because I love you! I continuously stand at your door waiting for your answer. I would love very much to come in and dine with you! If you repent and are faithful to me, I will grant you to be able to sit down with me on my throne. Would be just like me as I overcame and sat down with my Father on His throne. You need to listen to what the spirit says!

WHAT WILL WE SEE IN CHAPTER 4?

We see God on his throne in all of His glory before Jesus comes to His throne to his right hand. He is given glory and praise by the 4 living creatures and the 24 elders, as he was over all creation and all things that exist in heaven and on the earth.

Chapter 4

As Christ has come bringing salvation to the Gentiles and unto all men and with that message being carried by the apostles and other dispersed Christians, John sees a door standing open in heaven so that he could see God on his throne!

This appears to be before Christ comes to his right hand? Here is God on his magnificent throne with a rainbow around the throne! Breathtaking! The court seated around the throne, being the 24 elders in their white garments having been saved by the blood of the lamb with the crown of life on their heads. (James 1:12) This scene here may resemble the scene of Daniel 7: 9-10? Gods awesome power seen around his throne, as the seven lamps or the seven Spirits of God were before him! Before the throne was a "sea of glass", like crystal? The sea sometimes is used to symbolize many people and could it here refer to all the saved from all over the world? Rev. 7:14-15? Now in the center and around the throne were four living creatures which appear to be the "eyes of God"! Seems that each one had a distinct difference? Seems very diverse perhaps denoting what they do? A lion, mighty and fierce, a calf, domestic animal, perhaps gentle, one as a man, could be serving mankind? Then a flying eagle a powerful bird over the birds of the earth and the heavens? Remember God knows about the sparrows! Ezekiel 1 may be helpful to our understanding. They had plenty of eyes to see and wings to fly? They constantly were saying Holy, Holy, Holy is the Lord God the Almighty who was, and who is, and who is to come! The 24 elders seem to join in as they fall down to worship Him, even to casting their crowns before him! They too now give praise and glory to God who was so worthy! They acknowledge God's power as being over all creation, as it was his plan or will, that we all exist! (John 1:1-3)

WHAT WILL WE SEE IN CHAPTER 5?

Christ now comes to His throne to rule as our "King of Kings"! He is the only one that could ever be worthy to take the plan of God out of His hands and to carry it out. The 4 living creatures and the 24 elders worship him as he begins his reign!

Chapter 5

Now we come to the major part of this book as Christ has risen and now ascends to his throne at Gods right hand! As God sat on His throne He had a scroll that was written inside and on the back but sealed up with seven seals? Now a strong angel looks for someone who may be worthy to open the scroll and break its seals. At first it seems that no one in heaven was worthy to open the book and look into it. John starts to cry! Then one of the elders told him to stop crying because the lion from the tribe of Judah, the root of David has been resurrected/overcome and has come to heaven and is worthy to open the scroll with it seven seals. Now a lamb is seen among the living creatures and elders as having been slain. He has seven horns and seven eyes denoting his power of the ability of seeing all, he has been given all authority in heaven and on earth. Matt 28:18. He now takes the scroll out of Gods hand. As he does the four living creatures and twenty-four elders fall down before the lamb with all having golden bowls full of incense which were the prayers of the saints. It's a new day! They now sing a new song, praising Jesus who now comes to his throne to reign as our King. They praise him for his dying and bringing salvation to all men everywhere and for all people, through His dying and the shedding of His blood. His kingdom has now come and believers are made priest to reign upon the earth. (Colossians 1:13)

All of the host of heaven, too many to count, giving Christ praise and pronouncing Him worthy to receive such riches, wisdom, might, honor, glory and blessings. Then every created thing in heaven and on earth, even under the earth on the sea and all things in them, giving Christ blessings , honor, glory and dominion for ever and ever! The four living creatures agree He is worthy of all this praise with their amen! The twenty-four elders too, fall down and worship Him! What an awesome scene for John to see as Christ comes to His throne to rule over His "everlasting kingdom" which was promised so long ago. (Mark 9:1)

WHAT WILL WE SEE IN CHAPTER 6?

Christ now sets up His kingdom as he prepares to bring judgment to Israel and vengeance to the martyrs who cried out to Him. Opening the sixth seal the war and destruction is about to begin. The Romans and the rebellious Jews split apart, now ready to go to war with each other.

Chapter 6

With Christ now on his throne, He seems to set the kingdom in order to fulfill Gods plan for him. He involves the four living creatures in this and it may seem as each living creature is associated with a particular horse or work. Zechariah 6:2-8 may shed a little insight as to what this resembles or is about. His was about four horses patrolling the earth and seems to be doing things for him. The first we see is a white horse which possibly could be about those such as the apostles and others sent out to take the gospel to the whole known world before the end would come to the "Old Jerusalem"? (Matt 24:14) Bows were used and effective in battles in Old Testament and may signify the battles faced in proclaiming Christ to the world around them? The second living creatures now shows a red horse, that is to take peace from the earth, or it could be perhaps about what Jesus said that I did not come to bring peace (Matt10:34) or perhaps used in bringing judgment when it was needed? As the third seal is broken, the third living creature helped him to understand what it may be about. Here is a black horse with scales in his hand and may look to be in control of food and things to eat as it was to be a problem for the Jews, especially during the coming war with the Romans. Food to be very scarce and expensive! A days wages for a quart of wheat and also for 3 quarts of barley. But do not damage the oil and the wine? Could that be as it was used in the worship in the Temple? I want you to have it? As Christ now breaks the fourth seal the fourth living creature explains this ashen horse. The rider of this horse was given authority to kill one fourth of the earth. Seems to relate to what is about to happen as Gods plan calls for the destruction that is to come upon the Jews, Jerusalem and its temple. (Matt 23,24:2,21) To be the worst ever tribulation to come upon the earth! History says there were around 1 million people who were killed just in the city!

So bad the dead lay in the streets and men would have to climb over them. So it would be understandable that death and Hades followed him, awaiting these deaths. Now the Lamb breaks the fifth seal and we see the souls of the dead that lay beneath the altar. Having been sacrificed and slain because of the word of God and because of the testimony they had held on to which caused their deaths. They are ready for some vengeance and want to know, how long will it be?

Seems to be a priority which He deals with but is not to happen immediately. They were given a white robe and told to rest for a little while longer as there are more to be killed as they had been. There were a great number killed by Nero and other leaders and you could perhaps think about almost all of the apostles that was slain, even perhaps Steven who had lost his life? God would choose the right time, His time! Now the sixth seal is broken. Devastation begins, described as an earthquake. A time for weeping and mourning, with the moon becoming like blood. The worst ever punishment and destruction beginning. This would have been the time to flee to the mountains? So dark and with gloom, as the sun and moon would suggest, there to be tremendous bloodshed! The Jews had been and were rebellious against Rome but it had come to its head. The relationship of being peaceable and tolerant comes to an end. They are now split apart as those of places of rule and honor are taken out of their way, referred to as "mountains and islands". The war is on and in a major way. All men see what's happening and are very fearful. As Jesus was about to die, said, don't weep for me but for yourselves as destruction is about to come to you! You will be hiding in caves and in the mountains as this judgment comes. (Luke 23:28-31) The full-fledged war is now on and who is able to stand?

WHAT WILL WE SEE IN CHAPTER 7?

Before the war begins God takes care of a remnant of His chosen people. Jesus had earlier told them to flee to the mountains for safety. Other nations were warned also as they had been saved, wearing white robes, forgiven of sins. The world power, Rome, was bringing tribulation to Christians from around the world.

Chapter 7

W e see four angels about to begin the destruction that is to come in the war between the Romans and the Jews. But now we have to stop them as another angel comes down from the rising of the sun having the seal of God or approval to hold things up. He cries out with a loud voice that the war to happen between Rome and Israel be delayed for some time. Matthew 24:16 warns them to flee to the mountains to avoid death and for their protection. Seems similar to what was to happen in Daniel 12:1. This destruction held up by God, that first a remnant must be saved/protected. Also similar to Ezk 9:1-11. Do not harm the earth or the sea until we have sealed the bond-servants of our God. The men/women sealed and protected from all 12 tribes which would come to 144,000. Not literal but some from every tribe to be spared. Then we see the saved of the rest of the world, every nation, tribes, people and tongues that has now been saved by the blood of Christ proclaiming salvation as their King has also come. Remember Christ and the palm branches as he came into Jerusalem to be their King? (John 12:13) Angels now joining in with praise along with the elders plus the four living creatures. So happy in praises to God for the salvation that all men from every nation can now have! There is a little question as to where they came from?

Those of the world other than the Jews who has been saved by the blood of Christ, perhaps such as Melchizedek (Genesis 14:18) of whom even Abraham gave tithes to. Those of the world who had persevered through trials and tribulations. They now share in all of the blessings in Christ. (Rev 21,22) As Rome was the wicked world power these perhaps have been affected and gone through trials and hardships because of them? But now having overcome, they share in all of the blessings found in the "New Jerusalem". Christ now as their king can shepherd and guide them to "living water", never to thirst again. Also to dry up the tears in their eyes. All of the great spiritual blessings now to share together with all men, in the "New Jerusalem"!

WHAT WILL WE SEE IN CHAPTERS 8-11?

The next few chapters present a picture of the actual war from it's start to finish plus lots of other information as the mysteries of God finished!

WHAT WILL WE SEE IN CHAPTER 8?

Christ has his kingdom fully established and in order, so what does He do now? It may explain the silence for a little time or to their anticipation. Now seven angels given seven trumpets as the destruction of Israel begins. First in all of the land of Canaan and cities and finally to Jerusalem, which they thought would never again be destroyed.

Chapter 8

Christ now on His throne, having all power and authority (Matt 28:18), it seems to be the time for the four angels, who had stopped the process, may now have the green light as the seven angels are prepared to do this job, as they were given the seven trumpets. So now as the seventh seal was broken by the Lamb, heaven became silent for half an hour or meaning for a short time. Seems they don't know what's about to happen? Perhaps fear of what's to happen, maybe to include the end of the world? (I Cor 15:52) It's certainly not the end of the world but more than likely the end of the Jewish nation, Jerusalem and its temple. God's power now to be seen as the seven angels with the seven trumpets brings it to pass. This seems to be the answer to the prayers of 6:10-11. Also, to be the fulfillment of the prophecy of Jesus in Matt 24:29-31. Prayers to be answered with vengeance coming (Matt 23:34-36). The prayers go up before God. There may be significance as to where the fire comes from as vengeance now comes. From the altar, 6:9, from the souls of those who had been killed because of their faith in God and Christ. God's mighty power now to be seen! Vengeance now to begin! Angels now ready to begin. God's wrath and punishment now comes and may point to the starvation and famine that was ahead of them. It would eventually come to people eating their children as history reveals. (Matt 24:21) Food becomes very scarce as this war goes on for 3 1/2 years. The second angel sounded, seems to be about battles on the sea.

History reveals that the Jews had some great victories early on but as it looked bad for them, they thought going to the sea to fight them would be an advantage to them. So Rome/the beast jumps in! Turned out to be a bad decision for the Jews. The Romans sooner than expected overpowered them after coming up with needed ships. The sea became red and bloody as the Jews were killed and thrown overboard. These battles occurred in the Med Sea, out from Joppa and also some in the sea of Galilee. The men and ships were destroyed! The third angel sounded and a great star/angel fell from heaven burning like a torch and it brings torture and pain on the "rivers" and the "springs of water" which would be the Jewish people living out in the land. Rev 16:4-7 makes it clear as to who it is. The sinful/wicked Jews that had brought major suffering and pain to its own people. Two rebels, John and Simon, had many followers as they went through the land killing, robbing and taking all the food they could find. Many people came to fear these men more than they did the Romans! As wormwood, so bitter and hard to deal with. These days were dark and gloomy as they deal with their own, plus the Romans, as they are now winning. While it looks so bad and dark, a break in the war comes. There are problems in Rome and a stoppage of the war. An "eagle" flying in midheaven brings a message of this stoppage but it's not over because there are three woes to come. The eagle with the message seems to be from Rome as the "Eagle" was the Roman insignia that would go before their armies. Nero is dead and Rome needs a ruler! This will take 8 to 10 months for this to be settled. Two men, Galba and Ortho, attempt to come and take over this office, seemed to never gain control as they were soon killed.

Finally, Vespasian a great general over the Roman armies listens to his men who had tried to get him to go to Rome and take over this job. He finally goes and is successful! After things get better for him he sends his son Titus to finish the job of destroying the city and temple as he had won the battles out in the land. This is all that is left to take but Titus came not really wanting to destroy the city. He tried very hard to get them to surrender the city to him. The Jews, such a proud people, actually thought it could not happen to them, especially this city and its temple where God at one time had as "His city and dwelling"!

WHAT WILL WE SEE IN CHAPTER 9?

The fifth angel is about, Matt 24:21, the worst tribulation of all times! The worst ever! The Roman Jewish war is now stopped as their leader is dead. Thousands of wicked people as "locust", storm this little city, robbing and stealing the gold, silver and the food. Much worse torture then what Rome had done. An army of followers of John, Simon, Zealots, and Indumeans come into Jerusalem as the cities of which they has stolen and ravaged, had been destroyed by the Romans. So they all end up in Jerusalem for safety, gold and food. But Jerusalem was getting low on these things. It could have been up to 15,000 men coming into a very small city which was about a half mile wide, and one mile North to South. They could easily fit the description of locust as they destroyed it! Must read to get the picture, Ex 10:12-17! One of the devils angels had been cast down to the earth 12:9, and was given the key to the abyss, "City of Jerusalem". So wicked as so much torment going on in it! My dictionary on abyss : "original chaos, bottomless gulf or pit, an un-fathomable depth, as an abyss of sin:!" A perfect picture of that little walled in city! So his key opens the doors of that city to those locust/men, which was not about grass or green things but about men, women and children! It was God's plan and prophecy of Christ as he was given the keys to the city! The account of John being hard to understand but seems to be a way to see what the worst ever tribulation looked like. The sixth angel sounded as the rest of the land and cities about destroyed with only Jerusalem left.

Chapter 9

While Rome is getting a leader with no battles with the Jews. A star/Angel falls from Heaven with the key that opens the bottomless pit. These Locust will now be used to bring suffering to the Jews who at this time was free from the Romans wrath as they had stopped the war. As Locust the Zealots who had taken over the temple, the army/followers of John and Simon with their thousands of men have come within the city and brought the greatest pain ever to be given to any people! (Matt. 24:21) Only to torture those who do not have the seal of God on their forehead! This was a strange thing for the locusts/destroyers to do? This swarm of locust to bring a different kind of devastation. It was about stings and torment! Men were going to seek death and not find it! They will long to die but death flees from them. Seems with this, repentance and them turning back to God would have come. (Matt 24:21) To last for five months as this would be their normal lifespan. These evil men dressed up to disguise themselves even to dressing up as women with weapons hidden under their dress, plus having teeth as that of lions, so evil. Had protection or breastplates as of iron with the sound of their wings as the sound of chariot rushing to battle. They were everywhere! There were so many of them, could have been up to 15,000 among all of them? It's pure torture to have all of your food taken from you! As a scorpion with it's sting! The King or angel over them from the abyss, with the name of "destroyer or destruction". This is about vengeance unto those prophets that the Jewish people had rejected over the centuries and were killed for their faith in God and Christ. With all of that torture by the locust over, the four angels are now released as Titus is sent back by his father, now ruler, to finish the destruction of Jerusalem. He began to assemble his army around the Euphrates, in Caesarea. He had invited other nations to help him. His army now too big to count, armed and prepared to win this war. These four angels who had been waiting to do their job in destroying one third of all mankind, had the armies to do it with. The horses with the heads of lions, riders with breastplates with smoke and brimstone coming from their mouth! Very large and powerful! The rest of mankind not killed by this plague, would not repent of the works of their hands. The Jews were not about to give up as they still thought it would not happen to them!

WHAT WILL WE SEE IN CHAPTER 10?

It seems a decision in heaven is about to be made. We see an angel clothed in a cloud and a rainbow upon his head? Do we or do we not destroy Jerusalem now? A decision is made to go ahead, destroying the city and its temple and the mysteries of God are finished! Rev 10:7.

Chapter 10

God is always so good and faithful! Has so much patience but it seems it's about to run out on His sinful and rebellious people, Israel. Seems He may want to give them one more chance to repent? He had done it down through the years as they had killed the prophets and finally killing Christ who was to be their king.

The end of chapter 9 after such a slaughter that the rest still would not repent. The old law had been nailed to the cross and God's plan now is to destroy the "Old Jerusalem" as it had become an abomination to God as it was now the days of the "New Jerusalem". Now John sees a strong/powerful angel coming down out of heaven with his face like the sun and his feet as pillars of fire. Notice two things about him, he was clothed in a cloud and a rainbow was upon his head. Could this be about a choice about to be made? The cloud with thunder being about destruction or the rainbow where new hope is given or peace is made? Looks as if the decision is about to be made. He seems to have a message for them as he had an open book in his hand. He gave out a mighty cry and the seven peals of thunder uttered their voices. As John was about to write, a voice came from heaven saying, Seal up the things which the seven peals of thunder had spoken and do not write them. The angel that stands on the land and sea lifted his right hand to heaven and swore by Him who lives forever and was over creation that there would be no more delay. Now when the seventh angels voice is about to sound, the mystery of God is finished as the prophets have proclaimed. Christ now reigns with salvation to all men and the old laws are gone. Now the city and temple are about to go! This is about the prophecy of Isa, Jer, Ezk, Daniel, Zach, Christ and others. John ordered to go take the little book out of the angels hand and told to eat it. It was a good message and sweet in his mouth, but would be bitter in his stomach as it would not be obeyed! (Rev 9:20-21) Similar to Ezk 3:1-11. He ate it and it was good/sweet in his mouth but bitter on his stomach as they would not listen and repent. John then was told, you must prophecy again about many peoples, nations, tongues and kings, continuing your good work!

WHAT WILL WE SEE IN CHAPTER 11?

Efforts made for 3 1/2 years as the old law would be taught and protected that they might see and repent or give up. But we finally see the temple and the old law destroyed and coming to rest in the temple of God in Heaven. Christ now reigns as it is a new day for us.

Chapter 11

As we have just seen that John was told he would prophecy again concerning many peoples, nations, tongues and kings. So we begin now as John is instructed to go measure the temple of God, the altar and those who worship there. Something very similar happened in Old Testament that could help us in our understanding. (Ezk 40, 43:10-12) This seems to be for those inside Jerusalem with its temple, for those of the city? Leave out those not of the temple or city as they are given to the nations as the war goes on for 3 1/2 years. My two witnesses will prophesy for 3 1/2 years clothed in sackcloth, and in mourning? These are the two olive trees and the lampstands that they should have listened to and obeyed. God is providing and protecting them and their word during this time, keeping them from harm. They seem to be clearly identified as to who they were. They have the power to shut up the sky that it not rain, also with the the power to turn the water to blood and to cause many plagues to come upon their enemies. This was during the former days of their prophesying. We all would surely agree that this would identify them as Moses and Elijah. Same as Mark 9:4-5. When the 3 1/2 years is over, their testimony is over as the temple come to it's end. According to history around 1 million people lost their lives in this city and around its temple. The dead lay on top of one another! No doubt as to what city this is, it's where their Lord was crucified/ Jerusalem. As they lay in the streets they were not permitted to be laid in a tomb. This is actually referring to Moses and Elijah and their laws and prophecy destroyed. They had been hated over the years but now there is celebration that they are gone. What a scene with the dead bodies even on top of one another and not to be buried real soon. Also, the temple ravaged, destroyed and burned with all of its contents! Is this similar or perhaps a shadow of what happened as Christ lay in the grave? What was the status of the old law as it was nailed to the cross? They lay dead awaiting the call from God to "come up here". They went up into heaven in a cloud as their enemies watch them! In that hour there was a great earthquake! Remember Matthew 28:2 as Christ was raised, there was a great earthquake. The same earthquake pictured here as these two prophets were raised to heaven as the old law, Jerusalem and its temple was done away? Many killed with the rest terrified and gave glory to God of heaven. As the seventh angel sounded there were loud voices in heaven about the kingdom that has come and the old done away!

This is different, it's everlasting! Christ now our King and He will reign forever. Forever sounds so good as we have seen the destruction of the old. The 24 elders fell on their faces and worshipped God! We give thanks to God, the almighty, as Christ was and is now with all power and authority reigning over the "New Jerusalem"! Your wrath has come, judgement came for those who died as they were rewarded for their overcoming during these hard times. The word or the prophecy of Moses and Elijah, the old law now comes to rest in the temple in heaven as it was prepared to give it rest! You can imagine the celebration and the power of God seen here as the old law of God is finished and put to rest, and the new law coming into affect!

WHAT WILL WE SEE IN CHAPTERS 12-14?

The mysteries of God now finished! Now more information and learning about God's mysteries as they are unveiled. It goes all the way back to the birth of Christ as He was the center of all those mysteries. We now will see Him from His birth and through Him bringing judgment to Israel as He had promised or prophesied!

WHAT WILL WE SEE IN CHAPTER 12?

Thru a sign or explanation, we see Christ briefly from His birth until He is caught up to His throne. The woman, Israel, is fleeing to the mountains for safety! Christ wins the war in Heaven as the devil is cast down to the earth. Heaven is rejoicing as the devil is cast out with Christ reigning. God gives the devil 3 1/2 years to assist the Romans in this battle against Israel/Jews.

Chapter 12

Now we see a great "sign" in Heaven revealing more about God's plan to help us in our understanding of the mystery of God. Christ, coming through the lineage of David, is about to come into the world. This is another "sign" about His coming but given in a brief account. We see a picture of Roman rule with the devil working through them to persecute the woman/Israel. He stands before the woman awaiting His birth so that he may destroy Him. Remember, Matthew 2:16, of Herod as he tried desperately to kill Him. Christ is born, a male child as he would be the "King of Kings and Lord of Lords"! Just a very brief account of the life of Christ as Christ arose from the grave to God's right-hand to rule over His kingdom! The woman/Israel/remnant, to be cared for safely during this war with Rome and the Jews. 3 1/2 years. As Christ now comes to his throne, the devil now defeated, must go! There was a war in heaven over this with the devil losing! Defeated and thrown down out of Heaven, along with his angels. As the devil is thrown down out of heaven, there was a loud voice saying, salvation, power, the Kingdom of God, along with His authority has come! The devil, the accuser of our brethren has been thrown down. All men now able to overcome through the blood that Christ had shed! So many willing even to die because of the word of the testimony of Jesus. Those in heaven and on earth rejoice! But woe to the earth as he/devil has a short time and a mission to work with the Romans to bring Israel and Jerusalem to its end. As the devil came to realize he had been thrown down/defeated, he immediately goes after the woman/Israel through whom Christ had come. But the woman/remnant was taken care of during this war for a time, times and half a time. For 3 1/2 years he went after her with all of his might, flooding her with efforts to destroy her. It seems that the Jews out in the land were able to help defend her. The devil so enraged, as he is not able to destroy the woman, but now off to make war with the rest of her children, or those who are faithful to God and hold on to the testimony of Jesus!

WHAT WILL WE SEE IN CHAPTER 13?

God now uses the beast/Rome to bring judgment to Israel which was similar to the Babylon of old. The devil gave him his power and authority and also a two horn beast/false prophet to work with them in promoting the beast, forcing everyone to worship the beast or die.

Chapter 13

As the devil/Dragon has been cast down out of heaven, he now stands on the seashore waiting to team up with the beast/ Rome to work together in bringing Israel and Jerusalem down. We see the beast/Rome coming up out of the sea, the same beast that Daniel said would be ruling when all of this was to happen. Described as the world power of which it was. Shown to be very powerful and having great authority. (Daniel 7) Look what the devil did: he gave the beast his power and his throne and great authority. Seems as one of the emperors was dead, Julius, but replaced and all things back to normal. Agustus had restored Rome and back to its power? The devil/Dragon was worshipped as he had given his power to Rome. The people worshipped the beast and were in awe of him!

Augustus now dead and what seems to be the most wicked of all, "Nero" rules? There is no match for him. So wicked, but authority was given to him to destroy Israel, Jerusalem and its temple which was to take 42 months or 3 1/2 years. So he blasphemes, or speaks against, God, the tabernacle and its people. God had given Rome authority to go to war against the Saints and to destroy them as they were the world power at this time. Men from all over the world had now come to the place where they worshipped him. The Jewish nation is about to come to an end! Saints to have a severe test with many escaping, some captured and many killed. Now we see another beast/false prophet coming into the scene, he comes out of the earth and is much different from the other one. He had just two horns, not much power/strength but he spoke as a devil. He works together with the beast and devil, and given great authority. He now makes the Jews and the others worship the first beast that had been killed, Julius. He had the power given to him to deceive the people with the signs he could come up with, as he would perform them in the presence of the beast/his image! He told the world they needed to worship the image of the beast who had died and come to life. Seems to include all Roman rulers in these times? The beast with two horns/ false prophet, was able to make the image even to breathe and talk! He could speak and caused many who would not worship him to be killed! Then he demands that all men have a mark on them to identify them as his worshippers! If you don't have this mark, you can neither buy or sell. Many

Christians lost their lives as they would die rather than to worship him. The number could be calculated for the beast as it was a number as that of a man, 666. Nero?

WHAT WILL WE SEE IN CHAPTER 14?

Another review of the mystery as we always see the remnant protected first. Also we again see that the gospel has been preached to the whole world before the destruction comes. Matt 24:14. Now we see Christ coming in the clouds as we were told we would see. He has a sharp sickle in His hand to reap with, as the harvest is fully ripe. Does His love overcome vengeance as another angel was coming to bring destruction on the Jews, His chosen/the vine? Isa 5:1-7. The whole land is destroyed with much bloodshed! Again we have seen the mystery of Christ from His birth until He brings judgment to Israel! Mysteries finished!

Chapter 14

Now we take another look back to the time that the war was about to start. Things have been held up as the remnant was taken care of. (7:3-8) An awesome sound comes from heaven, the sound of harpists with the singing of a new song. This song was only for them, the remnant, as they were among the first ones to be saved by the blood of Christ. They sang the song before the four living creatures and the elders with no one else able at this time to sing it. They were the ones that have lived godly lives and now are following the lamb, having been purchased by His blood! First fruits to God and blameless! As you look at the prophecy of Jesus in Matthhew 24:14, the apostles and the disciples were to take the gospel to the whole world and then the end/destruction of Jerusalem would come. That seems to be what has happened here? That being done, now the hour of judgment is here. God is true, worship Him! All of you have now heard.

Another angel now saying as the timing is right that "Babylon the great" is to fall. She is so wicked and yet with so much pride! Babylon had been gone for many centuries but if you read Isaiah 47:1-10, think you can understand why Israel is called Babylon! So wicked and with so much pride. Israel is such a picture now of Babylon, being the "daughter" of Babylon. As the persecution comes from Rome, many will come to worship the beast or to die. Then what is to be worse is that some will submit and will be lost and condemned with judgment. Trying to get some to see if they die in faith, it would be so much better. It's going to be very hard but you must persevere! Yes, blessed are the dead who die in the Lord as you will receive your reward, a rest from all of your labors. Looks like Christ himself, now comes to bring judgment. He said that you would see him coming in the clouds in Matthew 24:30. This is it! The timing is just right as they are so wicked and deserve it. He does it over the earth/land. Another angel now appears to bring more destruction. Believe significant that he comes from the altar, that the dead lay under and had wanted vengeance. So it was to kill the Jews who in days of old have been called "the vine"! (Isa 5:1-7, Jer 2:21) Her grapes were ripe! So the angel gathered the clusters from the vine of the earth and threw them into the winepress of the wrath of God. These seem to be the wicked Jews out in the land of Canaan, which God had given them. The entire land was filled with blood as their wickedness was so great. The blood level was high and for a distance of the 200 miles. Measure it!! North to South? Only the city and the Temple remain to be destroyed after this.

WHAT WILL WE SEE IN CHAPTERS 15-16?

A third review as a sign is given back to the destruction of Israel and Jerusalem as the mysteries are finished. There is more information being given for a better understanding of the prophecy of Christ.

WHAT WILL WE SEE IN CHAPTER 15?

A *sign* is now given to help explain the seven angels with seven plagues coming shortly and the wrath of God is finished. Same as 10:7 that the mysteries of God is finished. Again first, the remnant saved and praising God. With the remnant safe the destruction now to begin.

Chapter 15

We may now go back to look and find more about what happened as the war between Rome and the Jews was about to begin. We see the 144,000 or remnant, plus the others from the multitudes of the whole world who has been saved by the blood of Christ. Pretty much similar to chapter 7:4-17? Now as we see the remnant,144,000, and the others of the world that have been saved by the blood of Christ, they together are like a sea glass to be tried by fire but will be victorious over the beast as they praise God. They sang of Moses and "the lamb" of the "New Jerusalem"! Their king has come as promised, righteous and true are your ways. All nations will come and worship before you according to the prophets. (Isa 2:2) The "Jews only" nation of God's people is no more! It's another look at the saved of Israel and the world that's about to be protected as the war is about to begin! Now we see the temple of the tabernacle of testimony in heaven open up. And Then we see the seven angels with the seven plagues that will bring destruction to Israel, Jerusalem and the temple as it seems they are ready to get on with it. One of the four living creatures gave to the seven angels, each their portion, seven golden bowls full of wrath of God. God's power is seen in the temple as it was filled with the glory of God! Their wait to begin this judgment is about over. No one could enter this temple until each angel and his plague were finished, or lastly, the old temple is burned up/destroyed forever!

Then, the old law and the prophets gone, they can "come up here" to their final rest before God! (11:12)

WHAT WILL WE SEE IN CHAPTER 16?

A short review of the actual destruction that came in chapters 8-11 by the same seven angels. Again, we see the wars beginning and all of the way to its end with even the walls being torn down! Matt 24:2. Babylon the great/ the great city/ Jerusalem comes to its end and is burned up as the other nations has joined in with them in the final destruction of the city.

Chapter 16

Now we go back to get a "second" look at the destruction of Israel and Jerusalem. This appears to be the same seven angels found in chapters 8-11. This account more brief but gives some more thoughts and meanings adding to our information and understanding. The first angel now reveals the beginning of the war and its destruction suggesting as to just who is receiving God's wrath and judgment. It seems on those who chose to worship the beast and its image throughout the land of Canaan. May want to compare 8:7. The second angel pours out his bowl into the sea and at all the deaths in the battles in the sea. The ships captured and all the men killed and thrown into the sea! Compare accounts in 8:8? Now the third angel pours out his bowl of wrath upon the "rivers and springs of waters" and they become as blood. This will reveal just who this is in the next verses. These were the ones that Christ had said would receive it, Matt

23:35. Jesus had told them this was coming upon them/ Jews as they had killed the prophets and others down through the years and would finally kill Christ! "They deserve it as those who were killed and lay under the altar cried out for vengeance"! Lord God Almighty, True and righteous are your judgments.

Compare 8:10-11. Now the fourth Angel pours out his wrath upon the sun so that it would scorch men with fire? This may refer to the famine as you would be killed and robbed of your food? It brought so much terror among those in the city as people wanted to die to get out of this misery! This brought so much darkness and gloom to this city! Compare 8:12. The fifth angel now pours out his bowl of wrath and looks at the problems that Rome now deals with. This would be during the delay in the war as was given in chapter 8:13. Both Rome, dealing with the death of their rulers, while at the same time so much pain and torture was going on in Jerusalem. The Zealots had taken over the temple, rebels, John and Simon, with their thousands of men bring pure terror in Jerusalem as they robbed and stole as food is about all gone. History says that some even ate their children! It was that bad! They brought more terror and pain than did the Romans. Yet, they would not give up or repent and seek God! Comparison with so much more said in 9:1-11. Now the Roman situation is worked out with Vespasion now ruler, sent his son back to Caesarea and around the Euphrates to plan on how to finish the job and to destroy Jerusalem.

The problems there now solved as they come to seek other nations to come and assist in this battle.

Vespasian, the emperor now, along with the devil and false prophet now reaches out for help. We are coming into Jerusalem as a thief to destroy it and those of the city, get ready, lest you be destroyed in it. As other nations join them they assemble together in a place called Har-Magedon, which was about 50 miles north of Jerusalem. Compare 9:13-21. Now the seventh and final angel poured out his bowl of wrath on them now in Jerusalem. Lets get it done! God's power is now seen. Seen as an awesome earthquake such as never seen before being so mighty. The answer to the prophecy of Christ that nothing like this has ever occurred and never would be again! Matt 24:21. There was a wall around the city with two walls within it, making it of three parts. Now one by one the walls were broken down and finally the temple is last to go. No more rule and power from within the city, as many priest and rulers were killed! Huge rocks/hailstones maybe bigger than a literal hundred pounds, come down on this city and walls that not a stone to be left upon another. (Matthew 24:2) The similar account in chapter 11:15-19 was more about the spiritual things than of the end of the Old Jerusalem. Christ is now reigning over the "New Jerusalem", His everlasting kingdom. Also a major part of the whole letter is about the vengeance that was to come to the slain for their faith in God!

WHAT WILL WE SEE IN CHAPTER 17?

The mysteries of the Harlot/woman that sat on the beast/Rome, who is she? The words she, her, woman, harlot, God's wife, queen, Babylon the great are all the same as Israel/Jerusalem/the woman! It has been a great mystery for many people. Rome did much in tolerating Israel with Herod even building some of the wall around it and also built a palace for Himself within the city! Jerusalem, loved by the whole world around her as they would come to that great city! But God's purpose for Rome was to destroy it as it had become so wicked. Rev 13:7. Also the temple worship to cease as Christ has come and the old law was nailed to the cross! Col 2:14

Chapter 17

Now one of the seven angels who had a part in the destruction of the Jews and old city now helps us in understanding better as to what has gone on. Described as a harlot/Israel, so sinful with lots of influence in the world. Seems that they may have become worse than the nations around them. The angel carries John, in spirit into a wilderness to show the relationship that the Jews had with Rome. Israel/Jerusalem had become rich but had become so sinful and like those around her. Just like Babylon the mighty nation, so sinful and with so much pride. Spiritually, she was Babylon! Identified by Isaiah 47:1 and Jeremiah 51:33 as the "daughter" of Babylon! Think that explains who verse 5 is? Israel had been responsible for the death of prophets and saints, even to the witness of Jesus.

John didn't seem to be sure of what he was seeing? So the angel begins to explain the mystery of this woman/ harlot and the beast/Rome that carries and helps her. The beast you saw is dead but about to come up out of the abyss to be destroyed. The world wonders how that could come about. Angels now explains to help clear things up. The seven heads/mountains identifies Rome as who carries the harlot/Jewish nation. Rome, originally described as having seven kings as now the 6th/Nero reigns. He is to reign yet for a little while. At his death, "Vespasion the 7th" will finish God's plan for the destruction of Israel and Jerusalem! So now it could be that the beast/Julius that had died, " his image, the 8th" as being one of the seven as his "image", will be destroyed? The 10 horns are the kings out in the territory ruling as they have been given areas/land to rule over. Would be those such as Herod and Agrippa? They may not last long in their rule but has power given them by the beast. They fight against the lamb, but he will eventually win out with a win over them. He is "Lord of Lords and King of Kings"! His army is the chosen and the faithful. It's plain as to who that the harlot is. Nations from all over the world, the emperor along with his helpers or kings, together, hate the harlot and will bring her to an end, destroyed by fire.

God is using them to accomplish his purpose as the prophets have said in His word. The woman, who you saw is the great city, "Jerusalem" where the Lord was crucified (11:8) and had much influence over the Kings and people of the earth!

WHAT WILL WE SEE IN CHAPTER 18?

Another angel from Heaven tells more of the mystery of Jerusalem/Babylon as it has been destroyed. Had plenty warnings but too proud as she said: "I sit as a queen and we'll never see mourning"! But there was mourning all over the world as their "great city" is gone. God had pronounced judgment to her similar to taking up a stone and throwing it into the sea, it's gone and not to be found any longer.

Chapter 18

Now we have another angel coming down from heaven, having great authority, the earth glowing from his glory. This is the fourth time we go back and look at what has happened. To show now that after Jerusalem's destruction, we can see some results of whats happened. Destroyed with no one able to live there! But a great place for demons, scavengers and hateful birds. It was because of how sinful they have become, just like all of the wicked nations around them. But it was not because they had no warnings. They have been told that it was coming to this generation by prophets and Jesus Christ. Matt 24:34. Her sins were great, piled up as high as the heavens. God is fed up and angry and will double the payback. She was very proud and living in luxury! She didn't believe that could happen to "her"! She was not a widow and would never be! She had come down so fast! One day was used to emphasize that it came quickly. God is behind this and He can get it done. It would have a great impact on the world around her.

They cry and weep that she is gone. This great city has received God's judgment in one "hour", so quickly! The merchants of the earth mourn as they have no one to buy their goods! Everything from gold, silver, silk, articles of ivory, things made from costly wood, bronze, marble, horses and chariots, even to slaves and human lives. Nowhere now to find and buy the luxuries that they have been able to get here. They all stand and weep! What will we do? Here again they can't believe how fast all of this great wealth is gone, one hour, again not literal. Actual time for this City's destruction was close to 4-5 months? Even to the ship masters as their living is affected by her destruction. There was no city like that city! People threw dust on their head, weeping and mourning because so many were made rich by her wealth, now so lost as it went down so quickly. But there are something positive about it as rejoicing comes from Heaven as saints, apostles and prophets get some vengeance as it comes for them. 6:10. "Your judgment has come and is well deserved"! To emphasize what has happened, a strong angel takes up a great millstone and throws it into the sea and we all understand how quickly it sinks down. This is a picture of Babylon/Jerusalem as she is destroyed so quickly! Gone forever! The great and glorious city that had so many things men would want to see and do there. A place for music and entertainment, but no more! Many crafts done there to be bought or sold, but no more! No light to be found from such devastation and it seemed to be a place people would go to get married, but no more! All of the great men of the earth, the merchants, had been deceived by their sin and deceitfulness. Again, a major reason for her destruction given again. Reference Luke 11:50-51, the blood of the prophets shed since the foundation of the word may be charged unto this generation!

Vengeance finally comes that was sought in 6:10!

WHAT WILL WE SEE IN CHAPTER 19?

Much is been seen of the old so now we look at the new. Heaven rejoices as God's mysteries are finished and settled. Jesus now reigning over His kingdom and the martyrs that lay under the altar now to receive vengeance! The marriage of the lamb has come as the Church of Jesus Christ is here and flourishing! We see Christ reigning over the earth as he brings judgment to Rome as Rome's emperor and his false prophets are cast into Hell, the second death. Rome is humbled and brought down. Daniel 8:23-25.

Chapter 19

For the fifth time we will look back at what has happened and its significance. With Christ now on his throne, His kingdom here, with the old law nailed to the cross, the old Jerusalem destroyed, the mystery is no more! The everlasting kingdom is here and it's now for all men, for all time or forever! A loud voice now says, "hallelujah, salvation, glory and power belongs to our God". This was the voice of a great multitude in heaven that understood that the judgment given to Jerusalem was true and righteous! She had become an abomination but now gone, his bondservants avenged. Again they say hallelujah! They are gone forever! Now the four living creatures and the 24 elders fall down to worship God saying "amen, hallelujah"! The voice from Heaven says praise to be given by His bondservants, including a great multitude as the sound of many waters/people all over the world/Saints to sound this "hallelujah" for the Lord our God, the almighty reigns. The marriage of the lamb has come that now we can see more clearly as the old law is gone. The reminders, the city and temple gone forever! We can rejoice! Christians are now living righteous lives made possible by the blood of Christ. So blessed are those who are invited to the marriage supper of the lamb! So great, so good, John fell at his feet in order to worship him that brings such good news! He refuses to be worshipped as he was a humble servant just as John. I'm just telling you about the testimony and prophecy of Jesus. Worship Him! Now we see in heaven, Christ, on a white horse as he begins to bring his prophecy to pass as, found in Matt,Mark and Luke, of His coming in judgment for Jerusalem and the Jewish nation. Clearly identified as faithful and true, he wore a robe dipped in blood, with his name being "The Word of God" (John 1:1). Had his army following him. Now ruling over his kingdom having become the "King of Kings and the Lord of Lords", as it was written on his robe and on his thigh. Seems Christ is now about to bring some destruction and judgment against the beast and some of his allies. The Jews had learned the hard way that Christ is King of Kings and had brought judgment on them. The Romans are now about to learn the same lesson as he brings judgment to them. They too will know that he is King of Kings and Lord of Lords." Hopefully we all get it"!! An angel cries out as he stands in the sun to the birds of the midheaven or sky to come and assemble for the great supper of God. They were to eat the flesh of kings, mighty men, the flesh of horses and those who sit on them, the flesh of all men, small and great. Looks like an awesome slaughter that will eventually come! Now you can see the beast and the kings of the earth preparing to make war against Christ and his army. God had used this beast, the false prophet and the devil/ dragon to accomplish his will of destruction to Israel. It has now been finished! Rome now comes into judgement as they continue to make war with Christ and His people. The beast and the false prophet who had aided him in deceiving many people in the worshiping of the image of the beast, the two now thrown alive into hell/the lake of fire that burns with brimstone! Many more killed along with them, by him/Christ who sat on the horse and the birds were filled with their flesh. Another victory for Christ! "King of Kings and Lord of Lords"!!

WHAT WILL WE SEE IN CHAPTER 20?

The Dragon/Satan having finished his 3 1/2 years of work in destroying Israel and the city, is now bound for 1000 years or for what we would call a long time! He could've already been loosed as we live in such a wicked world as it's already been almost 2000 years. Vengeance comes to the martyrs as they come to life and to reign with Christ for 1000 years or the long period we now live in. After this long time is over, satan is released and immediately persecutes God's people from all over the world. Similar to Gog and Magogs destruction as to what they were about to do, but God says no! God says enough and destroys the earth with fire! We then see a brief scene of the final judgment as the world has been destroyed. It's now Heaven or Hell for all men!! The judgement day!

Chapter 20

With God's plan of the destruction of Jerusalem done, death now comes to many Romans and to the beast or emperor and his image. The false prophet dead and thrown alive into hell, the other/third part/Satan is about to be dealt with. An angel comes down out of heaven to get this done as he has the key to unlock the abyss and a great chain to bind him with. He then is bound, thrown into the abyss for a thousand years. Not a literal thousand years but to emphasize for a long time. Being bound and thrown into the abyss has now limited his deceiving of the nations until the long time/ thousand years are completed. The devils influence and power still around though as his angels were thrown down with him when he was cast out of heaven (12:7-9). But after these things he will be released for a short time. Now we see thrones set up for judgment. Perhaps similar to what is seen in Daniel 7:9-10? It seems this court is about those that have been beheaded/killed because of the testimony of Jesus, and the Word of God. It's about those who would not deny God or Christ in the worship of an image before them or before losing their life. Vengeance is now served as those dead come to life to reign with Christ during this thousand years, or during this long period of time. It's 2020 now so it's already almost 2000 years since this message was given to John. This does not affect the rest of the dead, it's only for the martyrs who had died! This is the first of which have experienced this resurrection where the second death now has no power over you! With Christ now, reining with them for this 1000 years or a long time, final judgment/Hell will have no power over them! Would you say this is real vengeance? When this thousand years, or long time, are finished, he comes back deceiving the nations all over the world, but only for a short time. He has not changed! This would be similar to what had happened to Gog and Magog. (Ezk 38,39) They had come out to destroy God's people but God said it's not going to happen, as I am against you! So they were destroyed by God. So now here, we see Satan deceiving and trying to destroy God's people from the four corners of the world or the whole world. But God says it will not happen! So as satan surrounds the camp of the Christians/Saints the beloved city, the New Jerusalem, and fire comes down from heaven and destroys them! This is the "end of the world" and not the mere burning of a city! The devil is now cast into hell where the beast and false prophets had been thrown to be punished/tormented day and night throughout eternity. So now with the earth gone, destroyed by fire, we get a glimpse of the judgment, that so many scriptures have told us that would come. Now we see all of the dead, the great and the small as they stand before Him. Now the books are opened, one being the Book of Life, that all of us want to be in, while another book would contain the deeds that we had done. This is what we will be judged by. All of the dead of all time is here? Those in the sea, those of Hades were there, everyone to be judged according to their deeds! So now death and Hades are thrown into hell, the lake of fire as they are no longer needed! If your name or anyone's name was not found there in the book of life, would now be thrown into Hell/ Lake of fire to be forever and ever! This is such a brief look of the judgement at the end of the world but the fulfillment of so many prophesies about the end! Simple and clear!

WHAT WILL WE SEE IN CHAPTERS 21-22?

A picture of the "Paradise of God," our land of "Milk and Honey!" These are the blessings of the Kingdom that we now have in Christ! Rev2:7.

Christ's Kingdom has come as we are all in the last days or the "New Day" of Revelation. We see a picture of Christ and His bride/the Church as it has come down out of Heaven or is sent from God! One of the great mysteries of God's plan! Now in our days God and Christ dwell among us! It's about the spiritual blessings we enjoy today. It's not about physical things such as suffering, crying and pain. God uses the old "physical" Jerusalem to help us see our new spiritual Kingdom of Christ, His everlasting and more glorious Kingdom. Now God and Christ dwell among us giving us the only light we will ever need and is always available as the gates are never closed. These greater blessings and closeness to God are because of Christ and the shedding of His blood removing the sin that had separated us.

Chapter 21

In my study of the book of Revelation I see two main topics/points to consider that looms over the rest which is also very important! It's about the "mystery of God", in its completeness, revealed to us. Christ the root/descendent of David, 22:16, has come into the world rejected and killed by sinful men. He was buried but come forth from the grave on the third day and a few days later, came to be seated at the right hand of God. Abraham had been promised that through his seed, all the nations would be blessed as it turned out to be through Jesus Christ. His blood shed now, at the "right time", that all men, everywhere may be saved. He now rules as "King of Kings and Lord of Lords"! His everlasting kingdom has come and has been since Pentacost as Peter was given the keys/ gospel and was preached and obeyed. Christ lived and died under the old law and Jerusalem was the "city of God"! People from all over the world came here to worship! It's a new day, as some change has been made as the old law had been nailed to the cross, done away! The blood of bulls and goats could not do what the blood of Christ could do in forgiving sin! Through Christ all men from all nations under heaven have a new and better law. In this "new Jerusalem", one could have sins removed with a better relationship as we become "sons" of the almighty God. Throughout Revelation so much is said about the "old Jerusalem" but that the "new Jerusalem" is so much superior and now available, it's here!

The city of "old" had to go as they had become so wicked in rejecting their Savior and King, even killing him! We saw the destruction of the "old" as the Jews rebel, thinking that it could never come to them. I see the main points are about the old law coming to an end, with the "new Jerusalem", now the "city of God", flourishing by the blood of Christ and his new law. God's mystery is revealed, His complete will, and having looked at so much at the old, we now focus on the "new Jerusalem". Look at Rev 3:12, Hebrews 12:22-23, and even Isaiah looks ahead to this time (Isa 65:17-19). It's a new day, a new heaven and earth seen as there was no more sea! The seas in the world had always separated nations and people from one another but no more. That's over! We now can all be one in Christ. John now sees the holy city or "new Jerusalem" coming down out of heaven with the old heaven gone in the destruction of the old. Described as a bride, pure and clean and without sin, verse 9, the wife of the lamb or the actual Church? It's a new day with the tabernacle of God among and for all men, now to be His people as He dwells among us. In a spiritual sense, all tears are gone from our eyes or wiped away as they may still come at times. No longer a separation/death, no mourning or crying or pain as it is a new and better day.

The old law had been done away as it could not give us these greater blessings that are now given through Jesus Christ. Now God says from his throne, "I am making all things new". You must write it down, it needs to be understood"! It's done, finished, I am God/Alpha and Omega, the beginning and end! Salvation has come to all men who thirst for the water of life and without cost! He who overcomes will inherit these things as he has come to be one of my children.

Sons of God, how awesome! But for the unbelieving and sinful their part or inheritance will be the lake with fire and brimstone, the second death/hell! Now one of the angels that had a part in the destruction of the old says come here and I will show you the bride, the wife of the lamb. (Rev 19:7, Eph 2:21-22) John is now carried away in the spirit to a great and high mountain to be shown more about the holy city, the "new Jerusalem", coming down, heaven sent, and from God. Awesome! Having the glory of God with a brilliance of a very costly stone! It had a great and high wall with 12 gates, with an angel at each gate. Each gate had a name of one of the 12 tribes of

Israel. How awesome is that, as the old law was to bring us unto Christ. (Galatians 3:24) How "special" is it that the names of the ones who brought us to Christ to have their names on the "gates"! You see perfection and beauty with three gates on each side so that men can come into the city from the north, south, east and west, all men! Then the walls of the city had 12 foundation stones with names so appropriately named after the 12 apostles. How awesome is that as they had brought the gospel of Christ, the foundation being the death, burial and resurrection of Jesus Christ! Such a beautiful spiritual picture! This city is laid out in a square with length as great as its width of 1500 miles and also it's height, perfection! You can see the massive wall and understand In human measurements just how awesome it was, being 72 yards! The walls made of Jasper and the city was pure gold, clear glass! The foundation stones of the city/apostles were pictured as every kind of precious stone. The 12 gates were made of a single pearl with streets of pure gold! The old Jerusalem was as awesome as could be in its time but only a shadow of what we have in the spiritual city or "new Jerusalem"! No temple needed in this city as for God and Christ are its temple! They give all light with no need for the sun or moon as the glory of God gives it light and it's lamp is Christ, also having been it's lamb. Just as Jesus said, "I am the light of the world and no darkness is found in me"! (John 8:12) Now there is salvation for all men/nations and having been cleansed by the blood of Christ, now walk with God, their light, with directions from God and Christ. Night is no more, the gates never closed as God's invitation is forever open! You must repent of your sin, as sinners can not continue in that way, but being saved by the blood of Christ in obeying Him! Only those with their names written in the book of life, as they were saved! The saved, or we who have believed, enter that rest! (Heb. 4:3) This is the icing on the cake!

This chapter was about the "NEW JERUSALEM" which was actually "CHRIST AND HIS BRIDE"! Simply, "CHRIST'S BRIDE' which is the Church today, the "SPIRITUAL PARADISE OF GOD"! Rev. 2:7. What an awesome picture of the blessings we can now enjoy being part of the "BRIDE OF CHRIST"! "GOD'S FINAL MESSAGE," which we would surely be a part of! So now God gives us "HIS FINAL INVITATION" in chapter 22.

WHAT WILL WE SEE IN CHAPTER 22?

We see a "river" of the water of life that Christ had told the Samaritan woman that He would and could give her! The "river" may suggest there is plenty of this water and without cost. It has been made available to all men, all over the world! Now we have access to the "tree of life" as it is on both sides, being always available and accessible. As God's people, we also reign forever and ever! A great picture of an everlasting Kingdom! No more mystery!! John's book was written just before Jerusalem was about to be destroyed as they were not going to repent or change. The spirit and the bride/Church say come! Christ is the "morning star" as it is a "new day" in Him! A warning is given not to add to or to take away, anything from this prophecy! God's amazing plan now completed and revealed to us and to be studied and understood, and not a mystery any longer!

Chapter 22

Many people want to believe these last two chapters are a picture of Heaven. Hope to consider it now as a look at the "new Jerusalem", the bride of Christ or his Church! It seems to perhaps be a shadow of things to come as we finally get to Heaven? Remember the garden? Seems to be Paradise regained, only better! In addition to what we saw in chapter 21, we continue as we now have access to the "tree of life" and also to "living water" as we see the river of the water of life, coming down from the throne of God and of the lamb. This being about the everlasting kingdom of Christ as we don't have to thirst anymore! Our streams of the mountains are beautiful but no match for what is seen here! Now along side the river are the trees of life continually bearing fruit for every "month" so that by His grace we can eat and be healed of our sins. No longer any curse as we draw near to God as we serve Him." They will see His face and be known as

His children". It's all "day" now in the city of God as God and Christ are our light.

This is about the kingdom of God that's everlasting, that Christ said that some of them standing there would see in their lifetime. (Mark 9:1) He says these words are faithful and true and his angels sent to reveal this message. There is something here that is about to come about. But let's go back just a little as we have been looking at the "new Jerusalem" as it has come and as to what it's like. That had happened at Pentecost as Peter proclaimed for the first time as many people believed and obeyed. He goes on now to something to get ready for and it would be the destruction of the "old Jerusalem". He now reminds them again that this prophecy is about to be fulfilled! He is coming quickly, in that generation, and you will be blessed if you heed this prophecy of his book/word! John wants to worship this angel that has brought this message as it was so special! The angel would not let John worship him as he said, he was just a servant as John was, worship God! The angel now says to John, do not seal up these words of this book as the time is so near. His prophecy, especially found in Matt 23, 24, Luke 21, Mark 13 is to be fulfilled very soon! People are not going to change or repent, the filthy will still be filthy and the holy will still be holy. I am coming quickly and my reward is with me and you will be judged by your deeds. I am God, the first and the last, the beginning and the end. Blessed are those who obey as to be saved, who have washed their robes, been baptized (Acts 22:16) as they now have a right to "the tree of life" and may enter by the gates into this city, or "new Jerusalem"! Adam and Eve did not have this right! Outside are those who have rejected Me and would not give up their sinful ways. Christ now about to finish up says, "I sent my angel to testify these things that the churches would understand. Yes, I am the one, the root of David (II Samuel 7), the bright and morning star of the "new day of the new Jerusalem". He is the light of a new day! (II Peter 1:19) The Holy Spirit tells all men to come, we as the church wants all to come to this glorious new city. Those who hear and understands, come and obey. The one who is thirsty for salvation, come and drink the water of life that will remove all thirst! And it's without cost! You must not add to these words or plagues will be added unto you and if you take away from the words of this book, God will take your name out of the book of life, and the holy city, which this book was about! Christ says it's close, the time is near that I will come to destroy the old city. (Matthew 23:37-38; 24:34-35) The mystery of God, finished! What an amazing plan from God. Since Christ has come and died for us it's a new day in a new city of God, the "new Jerusalem", that is now!! It's truly special! Now God has given "HIS FINAL INVITATION" to become a part of the "BRIDE OF CHRIST"! Salvation now, today, and a hope of Heaven in the future! "THE SPIRIT AND THE BRIDE SAY COME". Chapters 21 and 22 are a great "LAST SERMON" and with "GOD'S LAST INVITATION " for us today!!

God's Mysteries Unveiled, Finished!

The "Apocalypse" or John's Revelation letter unveils the last of God's mysteries. It's an uncovering or unveiling of God's plan for man from the days of Jesus Christ down to the end of the world and through the judgment Day. It unveils the mysteries of the prophets in the Old Testament as they pointed to Christ and His kingdom that was to come. Even though they have now been revealed, I hope with this study we can come to a much better understanding of them. Its definition is about the mysteries and secret purposes of God, the root of the Old Testament prophecy. Now let us look back and we will see the mysteries as they have come to light and unveiled for us. We will start with a little of the old and all the way to the very end of all things. Jesus Christ was the center of all of the mysteries for thousands of years and we start as we look back to the mystery of his birth. We first look to Matthew 1:18-23 and to Luke 2:1-11. We see Jesus as he was born of a "virgin", coming into the world as the savior of man and would become "King of Kings" to rule over an everlasting kingdom. All of this was God's plan before the foundation of the world! 1Peter 1:18-21. It all began with someone "special" that would come into the world through the seed of Abraham in Gen 18:17-19, as God revealed this mystery to Abraham. God later appeared to King David and promised him that one of his descendants would come into the world to rein over an "everlasting" kingdom as his throne would be a established "forever"! 2 Sam 7: 12-16. Jesus then comes into the world and was rejected and killed. Matt 27:33-37 and Mark 15:22-26. Then he was buried. Matt 27:57-60 and Mark 15:42-46. But the grave could not hold him as he came forth from that grave on the third day.

Matt 28:1-7 and Mark 16:1-7. Then after he arose from the grave He lived among His disciples for some 50 days, teaching them the mysteries of the Kingdom that they had not fully grasped. It had been granted by God, that the 12 apostles would be able to understand the mystery of the Kingdom. Mat 13:11 and Lk 8:10. They would receive special knowledge of His kingdom as it was about to come. Jesus had taught them early on to pray that the kingdom would come. Matt 6:10. They would become God's servants and stewards of the mysteries of God.1 Cor 4:1. Then finally Jesus told Peter that he would give him the "keys" to the kingdom. Matt 16:19. The "keys", the mystery, turned out to be the "Gospel of Christ" that Peter preached to the multitudes at Pentecost in Acts 2. Christ had taken his seat at God's right-hand having received His power as the "King of Kings" and the "Lord of Lords". This fulfills the prophecy of Mark 9:1 as Christ had said "some of you will not taste death until you see the kingdom of God after it had come with great power". This power of God was seen in his preaching as it touched the hearts of those who had put Him to death. They wanted to know, what they could do? Now believing in the Christ that they had killed, 3000 souls were saved as they repented of their sins, were then baptized to have those sins forgiven, and receiving the gift of the Holy Spirit! Peters message at Pentecost solved forever the mystery of the kingdom/or Church as it was so clearly unveiled for us. Now being forgiven with the hope of Heaven as Christ blood had now saved them! Now with all of the blessings we have in Christ it is a new and better day! We are now a part of an everlasting Kingdom as Christ, our King, rules from the right hand of God.

As we move towards the mysteries of Revelation, let us stop in Hebrews to gain some knowledge that will help us in our understanding. It gives us an awesome contrast to see in the Old Testament and its laws and ways with the blessings we now have in Christ. With the old law gone, having been nailed to the cross, we are in the last days or the age of Christ and His grace, with a much better relationship with God! The contrast begins with Moses as he receives the old law from God on Mount Sinai. Now throughout the Old Testament and its prophets it's about the works of the law which they could not keep perfectly and which could not save man. The conscience of a man could never be completely cleared without the blood of Christ. Hebrew 9:9. It would only satisfy God until Christ would come. The blood of the bulls and goats could not take sins away. Hebrew 10:4. Also the old law and its ways seemed very hard for man to follow? But now in the last days of Christ it is a new and much better day! Hebrews will help us in the solving of some of the mysteries of their day which is also our days. But first let's go back to look at the prophecy of Isaiah as he looked forward to our day. Isaiah 65:17-19. It is the same blessings that we now have as we look at those in Revelations 21:1-5. Let's unveil all of this in order to come to appreciate God's plan for us, in Jesus Christ our King. It's not about heaven but about all of the blessing we now have as we will see later on! But looking to Hebrews as the old law is gone and the land of "milk and honey" is destroyed and burned up, we can look for greater things in Christ! It's our "milk and honey", our "rest". Hebrews 4:1-11. Verse four says that "we who have believed enter that "rest". We also noticed that the disobedient were not able to enter because of unbelief. Hebrews 3:18-19. What we have in Christ is so much greater than their land of "milk and honey".

In Christ now there remains a "rest" for us and it's for us "today"! Hebrews 4:7-11. Is about obedience to the gospel of Jesus Christ as we "rest" from the works of the old law as we live in the last days, the age of Christ and of His grace! Christ paid a tremendous price in His death to provide this "rest". Hebrews 4:16. Now let us draw near with confidence, to the throne of grace so that we may receive mercy and find grace to help in our times of need! We now have "Hope" as the anchor of our soul both sure and steadfast and enters within the veil where Jesus has entered as a forerunner for us. He has become our High Priest forever according to the order of Melchisadek. Hebrews 6:19-20. Hebrews 8 & 9 tells us more about our covenant with God which is so much greater with greater promises. In Christ, our King, we now through His death have the forgiveness of sin and our conscious wiped clean which the blood of bulls and goats could not do. The old law would only satisfy God as He knew the future as Christ would come to provide it. Now, Hebrews 12:22-24 begins to unveil much more about our "milk and honey" or our "rest"! In Christ now we have come to Mount Zion and to the city of the living God! More special as it is an everlasting, heavenly Jerusalem! Remember Jesus said that His Kingdom would be different and not like those of the world around us. John 18:36. It has become the eternal city, unshakable with all of its myriads of Angels where God dwells among us and will be forever. This Kingdom is the very same thing as the assembly and Church of Jesus Christ. The first born who are enrolled in Heaven and to God the judge of all and to the spirits of the righteous made "perfect". That's about the men of faith in Chapter 11, of the old law and the old world, now have the blood of Jesus applied to them finally making their conscience clean and perfect! Now Christ is before God also as our mediator with his blood being sprinkled for us that is so much better than the old covenant, now with our sins gone! Now as we look to Revelation we see the unveiling of all the mysteries, except for one. Jesus said in Matthew 24:36 that no one knows the mystery or the day when Christ comes back but God Himself. Not even the angels, nor his Son. In Revelation, mysteries are unveiled as Christ comes to His throne at God's right hand. God has a scroll in his hand that no one can open but his son Jesus, who now comes to reign. All the host of heaven pronounce Him worthy to open the book with it seven seals. Also, the angels along with every created thing on earth and even under the earth, give praises, honor, blessings and dominion as His everlasting Kingdom has come. They all now worship Christ! Most of the book of Revelation is about the destruction of Jerusalem along with its temple and the old law going away as it was nailed to the cross. Now is very significant as it is a new day as Christ reigns! As the seventh angel would sound Christ had completed and finished what we would call His cabinet and His staff to get His things done with one thing being the destruction of Israel, Jerusalem and the temple. Everything now in place to accomplish His will and work. That may explain the silence of 1/2 an hour anticipating the first moves of Christ as he takes over. As when we go on through the war, beginning in chapter 8 in coming near to the end we need to look at Revelation 10:7 as it says that when the seventh angels sounded "the mystery of God is finished", as he preached to his servants, the prophets. So now we go to Revelation 11:15-19 to see what this mystery was. The most important thing is that Christ is ruling over His Kingdom and is about to bring about the end of the nation of Israel as he brings judgment/destruction to them. Christ is the center of this mystery, as he was given all power and authority. Matthew 28:18. His Kingdom is different as he rules from Heaven. It's a spiritual Kingdom that will never be destroyed. It's a shame that it's still a mystery for much of the world around us today! He reigns forever and ever, now, and "today"! What might be a mystery too here is that Heaven worships and praises God as he has fulfilled his prophecy of Jesus in judging Israel, giving vengeance to those who have died, in giving their lives when threatened with death. Christ had said it goes all the way back to the Old Testament to Able and down through the centuries of many prophets who have died and finally to Jesus Christ. Matthew 23:35-36. What could be mystery three that was finished, it's about the old law gone and now the ark of the covenant, that came from the temple as it was just destroyed now comes to "rest" in the temple of God In Heaven. Rev.11:19 We now have a more superior and greater covenant with better laws and promises. Mysteries finished! Chapter 17 has so much about mysteries so let's look at those! "Babylon", who is she? Surely enough given here to have a clear understanding of who Babylon is? A great harlot should almost give us the answer and it helps us in describing "Israel" as they had turned away from God! Many times in Jeremiah and Ezekiel, Israel was called a harlot. Jer 2:20, 3:1-8., Ezk 16:15-17, 30-38. Israel was also called an "adultress wife" as she had been Gods wife. Israel also call the Daughter of Babylon in Isa 47:1-5, Jer 50:42, 51:33. People from all over the world love Jerusalem and came there. Described her as she was carried by the beast/Rome. It was a rich and immoral city. In chapter 17:5 it should be plain as day as on her forehead she had her name: a mystery, "BABYLON THE GREAT THE MOTHER OF HARLOTS AND

REVELATION: the New Jerusalem is Now!

OF THE ABOMINATIONS OF THE EARTH"! It was such a wicked city where our Lord was crucified and where Jesus had said that judgement would come upon "you"! Matthew 23:34-36. Israel was a perfect picture of the Babylon of old as she was so wicked, proud, thought of herself as indestructible. In a spiritual way (mystery) Israel was just like Babylon! Being so rich, proud and thinking God would not let them be destroyed again could easily look like the daughter of Babylon. In Rev 18:7-8 she glorifies herself and lived sensually to the same degree and said in her heart, "I sit a queen, I'm not a widow and will never see mourning". It's the same attitude found in Isa 47:7 as she said" I will be a queen forever". In Zep 2:15, the proud city which dwells surely, who stays in her heart," I am and there is no one besides me"! The Angel unveils more to make it plain that the mystery "Babylon", was about the destruction of Jerusalem and its temple! It was Gods plan as Rome was prophesied in Daniel 12 that it would be the world power to have 3 1/2 years destroying the land, city and temple. They will hate the harlot/Israel, make her desolate and naked, eat her flesh then burned her up with fire! This is common purpose given to the beast as God's word was fulfilled as this woman or great city was destroyed according to God's plans. A look at the mystery of the "abomination" that brought on the "desolation" of Jerusalem! This is the abomination that Christ warned them about, and the same abomination that Daniel foretold in Daniel 12:11. Destruction was about to come and they would have an

102

opportunity to get out and flee to the mountains. Matt 24:15, Lk 21:20-22. A band of evil men from all over, named Zealots, came into the city and took over the temple! Not so large and number, they sought after the indumeans from nearby to come in and help them as they had so much opposition. With their thousands of men, and together they killed priest and all of the more prominent men of the temple even making some of their own men priest, mocking, as they knew nothing about the priesthood! Worship was profaned and even stopped as they would not let the Romans or anyone else come in to make a sacrifice. As the desolation was about to come, Luke says that now as you see the city beginning to be surrounded by the Romans you must flee to the mountains as the desolation is near. Hope that mystery is no more, but clearly seen! Rev 13:2 unveils the devil giving the beast/Rome his power and authority, also the false prophet as he works with them to get this destruction done. The mystery "Babylon" clearly seen as the harlot, Israel, God's adulteress, unfaithful wife who would be destroyed by the beast, Rome!

Most of the book of Revelation has been about the mystery and significance of the destruction of Jerusalem and its temple. It's now a new day in Christ with the old law gone as it comes to rest in heaven. Now we look to the fulfilling of Isaiah's prophecy in 65:17-19. "Behold I create a new heaven and a new earth as the former things (the old law") will not be remembered or come to mind.

So be glad and rejoice forever in what I create. For behold I create a "new" Jerusalem for rejoicing and to her people for gladness" I will also rejoice in Jerusalem and be glad in my people and there will no longer be heard in Her the voice of weeping and the sound of crying. This prophecy of Isaiah was looking ahead to our day or in the last days as Jesus had come to reign. It's about the "Rest" we now have that is so much greater then their "milk and honey"! Now to Rev 21:1-4 as it is almost exactly like what Isaiah wrote as we again see a "new heaven and a new earth" as the old city and its laws of the Old Testament done away and destroyed. There was no more sea as Christ has come to save all men from all over the world for all time! We see the holy city," New Jerusalem" coming down "out" of heaven. Mystery? It's about Christ coming down out of heaven to meet his bride, the Church! It's all about now, "today". It's here and yet as glorious as it is, it's only a shadow of Heaven. Now the tabernacle of God is among men "on the earth" with God and Christ dwelling among us as we are now His chosen people or the "New Jerusalem". Gal 6:16. As Isaiah said God will now wipe away every tear from our eyes. It does not mean that we will have no tears but we can overcome our sorrows of the world and the sting of death through faith in Jesus Christ!

Now we are a part of an everlasting Kingdom that means there is no death or separation from God as we are spiritually free from mourning, crying or pain, as the old way of such is gone. Jesus said as He was about to die that they not weep for Him but perhaps saying that you may have tears for those who have no hope. Our hope in Jesus Christ can and does wipe away our tears! Again, write it down as it is a "new day"! He said "it is done!" The mystery is now completed and finished. We have the great blessing that if we are thirsty for Christ, He gives us water from the springs of the water of life, without cost! Christ and His suffering and death has already paid the price for us! He who overcomes the world will inherit these things and he will be God's son as He has adopted us into his family! Those who continue to live in sin cannot have these blessings as their part will be in the lake of fire and brimstone which is the second death. Now one of the seven angels that had a part in the destruction of Jerusalem and its temple says to John to come here and I will show you the Bride, the wife of Jesus the lamb, giving more information about these great mysteries! He uses an analogy of the old city that was destroyed but rebuilt into an everlasting city the "New Jerusalem" which was so beautiful and perfect. He uses the most precious things of the world such as gold and silver, jewels and stones to make us see how special the "New Jerusalem" really is! But, it is still only a shadow of what heaven will be like! Peter had said that the best we have and know about, such as gold and silver is perishable. Our "New Jerusalem" is an eternal or everlasting city that will not pass away nor can it be burned up. In verse 21:10, again

John was shown the Holy City, "New Jerusalem", that had come down out of the heaven!

It's more about the mystery of Christ and His bride, His church in all of her brilliance! A gate and high wall with 12 gates. There were 12 angels at the gates with the names of the 12 tribes of Israel on each gate. How appropriate and awesome is it that their names would be on the gates of the city as the old law that is now gone which was given to bring us to Christ or to the entrance or gates. It was our tutor or schoolmaster to bring us to Christ. The angel had a measuring rod to measure the city. It was laid out in a square with it's length and width the same as 1500 miles or very large to our minds. The walls were huge at 72 yards which would be indestructible! Remember the old that Jesus said there would not be left one stone upon another as it would be destroyed. Matt 24:2. That's exactly what happened. This city was as pure gold like clear glass. The foundation stones were made up of the expensive and precious stones of the world. The 12 stones representing the apostles and the gospel they had taught and was to take to all of the world. The foundation of Christ, his death and resurrection to life reigning over his Kingdom. Each of the 12 gates were made up of large single pearl in the streets of the city as transparent gold. Would be hard to imagine anything being close to being of such great beauty. In this "New Jerusalem" there was no temple? The Almighty God and his son, Jesus Christ, are its temple! No sun or moon needed as the glory of God gave all of the light needed along with its lamp, Jesus Christ. People from all over the world now walk by this light and the kings of the earth brings their glory an honor into it.The gates are always open as God's invitation is always available to those who want to enter the city. Only those who are obedient to God can enter as their names are written in the Lambs "book of life"! Chapter 22 continues with the mystery of the "New Heaven and Earth"! It unveils more of the great blessings we now have in the last days of Jesus Christ and His "bride, the Church"! We see a beautiful picture of the river of the water of life coming down from the throne of God and the Lamb. This is what Jesus was telling the Samaritan woman at the well that he could give her "living water"! What a picture with the tree of life on both sides of the river bearing 12 kinds of fruit for every month of the year with its leaves for the healing of the nations. No more curse for those who serve him. Now with sin gone and a closer relationship with God as we now can see his face and we will be identified as His children. No more light needed as God and Christ are our light as we reign with Him forever and ever. He ends the book as He started it as the judgment to Israel is about to happen or it is very close. In a very short time now Israel and Jerusalem will be destroyed as I am coming quickly and blessed are those who heeds the words of this prophecy. John again wants to worship the angel as this great message had overwhelmed him but was told not to, and that he needed to worship God, as he was just a fellow servant. So now don't seal up the words of this prophecy for the time for the judgment of Christ has come. The people are not going to change! The lost are still going to be lost and the righteous will still keep himself whole and saved. You will be rewarded for the works you have done. Christ now says, "I am Alpha and Omega, the first and last, the beginning and the end". I am God the creator of all! Blessed are those who wash their robes in order to have the right to the tree of life and may enter by the gates into the city, the "New Jerusalem"! The immoral and sinners cannot come into the city as they have not been saved. Jesus, the descendent of David had sent His angels to reveal his word to John. He identifies himself as the "Morning Star"! We said many times it's a new day that he is bringing or the dawning of a new day! Jesus is the light, the new "Morning Star". He has brought salvation to all men from all over the world or Earth. Yes, it's a new day in Christ as the old laws and ways are gone. The spirit and the church/Bride say come and be a part of us as the invitation still stands. Let the one who hears also say come. Let the one who is thirsty come and drink of the water of life that is free and without cost as Christ had died and paid it for us. The mysteries of God now revealed/unveiled as we have been given all things that pertains unto life and godliness.2Peter 1:3. We still don't know the mystery of the day that Christ will come in his glory to take us to heaven to be with God. We only need to be ready and prepared for whenever it is! As we come to the final words of John's letter there are words of warning for us as we are told you don't add to nor do you take away from Gods word. Always remember, God's word is higher and better than ours and we will be judged by His word. We are going to have to please and satisfy Him and be careful not to use mans wisdom which would cause us to be lost. God's mysteries finished!!

The greatest mystery in Revelation that we need to understand is "THE NEW JERUSALEM THAT HAS COME DOWN OUT OF HEAVEN"!! Revelation 21-22:5 gives us a picture of a "new Heaven and a new Earth" as the old Jerusalem has been destroyed by God for a SECOND TIME! Jesus still loved His people, so remember as He was dying on the cross, He said: "Father forgive them, as they do not know what they are doing." So He now says, "I'm giving you something so much greater than a NEW JERUSALEM that's a SPIRITUAL CITY, an ETERNAL CITY THAT CANNOT BE DESTROYED!! A city where God and Christ will dwell among you forever!! AMAZING that the last two chapters of Isaiah and Revelation are about the "New Jerusalem" and is the same as the "Heavenly Jerusalem" of Hebrews 12:22-24! Christ now rules and reigns over His Everlasting Kingdom, which is another great mystery! Now with the Old Law gone, Paradise is restored, in Jesus Christ! No more death as we have access to the Tree of Life, eating bread to never hunger and drinking water to never thirst! God's mysteries finished and unveiled! the "NEW JERUSALEM" is HERE, NOW, TODAY!!

EPILOGUE

I feel so blessed to have had the opportunity to do an extensive study of the book of revelation. It's a shame it had to happen in the latter part of my life. It happened in a strange way as God does things in ways hard for us to understand with my wife having medical/physical problems requiring me to be home close to her in order to take care of her needs. Having retired and working with seniors, I had to give that up to care for her. It turned out to be at least two major blessings for me! The blessing of taking care of the most loving person ever known, that had became to be my wife. Such a rock for me down through the years as she could never do enough for me as her husband! Her faith in God never wavered as she went through all of her trials and suffering. As I needed to be close to her, I came to have more free time of which came to be a blessing!

More time for Bible study! Didn't know much and having not studied it as I should have, I was challenged to work with Revelation as I felt God had not given us something we could not understand. Mornings were my best time always to get things done, because my wife's needs were not so great in most of them. What a blessing given to me with that time to get this done! During her needs of 5+ years I gave this study most of my attention. Gods "mystery" "had been revealed", with God's complete plan now here for us to understand. Would never say I came close to understanding all of it as I'm still learning. What this study is about is the "context" of the book! I could never give all the specific details that are so difficult. Hopefully enough to maintain the context throughout the book. Hoping to stimulate all of us to a more and better understanding as we can study more as we grow in our knowledge of His word. My study allowed me to take care of my wife, almost exclusively at home, which was something we were both most happy about! As I began and gained more knowledge of Gods word, this book came to bring me more excitement than I ever had! I had never even thought of writing my understanding down to maybe share with others to excite them as it has me. It's finally come to the point of where I feel I am compelled to do so! With so much misunderstanding of this book, I was hoping this might stimulate others and their faith. You may notice I have a lot of question marks which is used as I cannot always be adamant of its meaning but certainly looks worthy of consideration. There is a possibility I could be wrong in some areas of question marks. They seem logical and I feel I have given significant scripture to support my views. The "new Jerusalem" is here and I hope and pray these notes, with my understanding can excite and bless others as we come to know Gods complete plan or what was for so many years a "mystery". Hopefully now we all can pass this message on to be shared with the world around us. It is so awesome and how He gets all things done is truly amazing! The "new Jerusalem" is even more amazing and I hope it will inspire all of us to be a part of it, and to share in it with the world around us!